IT IS A GLORY TO HER

IT IS A GLORY TO HER:
HOW PORNOGRAPHY IS MISOGYNIST AND PURITY IS PRECIOUS

TIMOTHY L. FAN

Published by God-centered Universe Press
www.gcupress.com

ISBN-13: 978-0-9981369-1-2

"*And such were some of you. But you were washed,
but you were sanctified, but you were justified in the
name of the Lord Jesus and by the Spirit of our
God.*" (1 Corinthians 6:11)

CONTENTS

PREFACE

Dear Reader,

In many respects, the way in which men view and act towards women defines the measure of the general morality of the particular age in which they live. As such, we, like Ezra, the scribe of old, tear our garments and our robes, pluck out some of the hair of our heads and beards, and sit down astonished, for ours is a wicked and adulterous generation. Without repentance, the unabashed misogyny of today's men, coupled with the immodesty of today's women, only assures our current society of the divine wrath. Therefore, as we begin this tract—it being a short, yet immensely urgent reflection on God's design for the glory of Christian purity—we come repenting, praying with Ezra:

> *And I said: "O my God, I am too ashamed and humiliated to lift up my face to You, my God; for our iniquities have risen higher than our heads, and our guilt has grown up to the heavens....O LORD God of Israel, You are righteous, for we are left as a remnant, as it is this day. Here we are before You, in our guilt, though no one can stand before You because of this!"* (Ezra 9:6, 15)

You are precious to Him who shed His blood for your purity!

In Christ's Covenantal Love,

Timothy L. Fan
Aurora, Colorado (Palm Sunday 2018)

TO MY PRECIOUS, LITTLE "PROMISE"

"By faith I saw the Lamb of God…." May the Lord make you as pure as Elizabeth, as meek as Mary, as humble as your namesake, and as God-fearing as your own, beloved mother. You are ever so precious to Daddy. (2 Peter 1:4)

1

GOD LOVES WOMEN

GOD loves women. For, He specially created them in His own image, in His own likeness:

> *God created man in His own image;*
> *in the image of God He created him;*
> *male **and female** He created them.*
> (Genesis 1:27)

On March 7, 1901, at about 6:30 in the morning, Amy Carmichael was greeted in her missionary bungalow in Pannaivilai, a village near the very southern tip of India, by a Christian woman and a desperate, seven-year-old girl. The Christian woman had bumped into the girl during the girl's daring, second flight from bondage as a "temple child" dedicated to one of the Hindu gods. (After her first attempt to escape, she had been branded with hot irons.) Having heard rumors of a missionary woman (Amy Carmichael) who loved children and who was called "Missie Ammal," the girl had fled in search of her, and had requested that this Christian woman, whom she had encountered the previous evening outside of a church, take her to her at once.

The girl's name was Preena. God saved her. He saved her via the evangelistic love of Amy Carmichael, who immediately adopted her and became her "Ammai," her "true mother." In Preena's own words, written fifty years after the event, "From that day she became my mother, body and soul."[i]

Yet what was it out of which Preena was saved? Certainly, she was saved out of her own *spiritual* slavery to sin, and thus her own *spiritual* condemnation, through the eternal Gospel, which her new "Ammai" so lovingly taught to her. For, the love of Christ Jesus was so strong in the soul of Amy Carmichael that her adopted children could sense it in her presence and see it in her eyes.

However, Preena was also saved out of an extremely diabolical form of *physical* bondage. For, had she remained in her training in singing and dancing in the Hindu temple, as a "temple child," she would have grown up and discovered, to her horror, that all of her training was aimed at *forced temple prostitution*. That is, she had been the victim of Hindu-temple sex trafficking, even at such a young age.

Once Preena's story became clear to Amy Carmichael, thanks to Preena's openness and honesty regarding all of the things that she had seen and heard within the house of the "temple woman" (as the woman in charge of the "temple children" was called), the bold missionary from Missisle, Ireland, was simultaneously overwhelmed by sorrow

2

and moved to action. Since this type of child sex trafficking (for service to the temple "god") successfully had been kept hidden from the view of expatriates in India, it was heart-rending news to Amy and to her missionary team.

Praying for God's revelation of the source of such crimes against little girls, Amy and her missionary band labored hard to discover the truth. How did such precious little ones end up enslaved to such a wicked system of abuse? Most of them were sold into it by their own parents. For instance, the parents might promise to "dedicate" one of their children to the temple "god" if the "god" would cure a severe sickness that was in their home. Or, an impoverished mother might sell her little daughter to the temple as a supposed "happy" economic arrangement for both mother and daughter.

The exposure of this kind of wickedness committed against little girls moved Amy to tears of anguish. It became her cross for the remainder of her life. This is what led up to her now famous prayer-time vision of Jesus, weeping over His own suffering children:

> Sometimes it was as if I saw the Lord Jesus Christ kneeling alone, as He knelt long ago under the olive trees. The trees were tamarind now, the tamarinds that I see as I look up from this writing. And the only thing that one who cared could do, was to go softly and kneel down beside Him, so that He would not be alone in His sorrow over the little children.[ii]

For anyone who loves the personhood and humanity of little children, Amy Carmichael's discovery of forced Hindu-temple prostitution (and yet it was God who enabled her to expose it) is a fatal blow to the so-called "goodness" of the "gods" of such Hindu temples. At the same time, it raises the overarching ethical question of prostitution, itself. Is not prostitution evil? Is it not dehumanizing to women, and that in one of the greatest measures? Is it not, then, *misogynist* (woman hating)?

Since God *loves* women, He *hates* the abuse and degradation of women. Thus God has set forth in His holy Law many commandments which serve to protect women from violence and exploitation at the hands of wicked men. For example, if a man in ancient Israel were to sell his daughter into prostitution, that man would be guilty of *a capital crime* (Leviticus 19:29, given in the context of capital crimes). Also, the crime of rape is recorded in the Bible amongst the kinds of sins that are so diabolically grave as to merit swift and immediate *capital punishment* (Deuteronomy 22:25).

God loves women, and, therefore, He honors those women who fear Him with high honors in Holy Scripture. Thus the earliest announcement in the Bible of the Gospel of salvation from sin and death comes in the form of a prophecy about *the woman's "Seed"* crushing the head of Satan, the Serpent of old:

*"And I will put enmity between you and **the woman**, and between your seed and **her Seed**; He shall bruise your head, and you shall bruise His heel."*
(Genesis 3:15)

Christ Jesus, the Son of God, is the woman's *"Seed."* Born of the virgin Mary, being fully God and fully Man (eternal in His Godhood, uncreated, without beginning or end, and yet the One who took on flesh and dwelt among us in the Person of Jesus of Nazareth), He alone has the power to break the curse of sin and death. For, being born of a virgin (He can have no true human father, since God is His Father), His blood, shed on the cross at Calvary, alone possesses the divine worth to make satisfaction for our sins against God (for only *divine* blood can pay the justice price for the sins of the whole world). At the same time, since Jesus is born *of a woman*, *of Mary*, His assumption of a full human nature means that He is able to be the substitutionary Lamb, the sinless sacrifice for the forgiveness of our sins (for only a truly *human* Messiah can die in the stead of other *humans*, and thus bear God's wrath against *human* sins).

Moreover, even at His resurrection from the dead on the third day (first having been crucified, dead, and buried in the tomb), Christ Jesus chooses to honor *the women* amongst His disciples, first. He bestows upon them the honor of being the first human witnesses to His resurrection from the grave. Their witness is *not credible*, in the Roman sense, since in ancient Rome a woman's legal witness is highly devalued. Yet the fact that they are, indeed, the first witnesses to the resurrection of Christ makes the Gospel accounts, written by Matthew, Mark, Luke, and John, *historically credible* (for who would forge such a story, at the risk of his own life, and yet make women the first witnesses to the resurrection in a society that highly devalues the legal witness of women?):

> *Yes, and certain **women** of our company,*
> *who arrived at the tomb early, astonished us.*
> *When they did not find His body,*
> *they came saying that they had also seen*
> *a vision of angels who said He was alive.*
> (Luke 24:22–23)

What, then, makes a woman valuable? Is it immodest, seductive clothing—ever so fashionable—that catches the eyes of lustful men? Is it intellectual savvy, proving that women are just as smart and capable as men in areas of rational and scientific inquiry? Is it not, rather, God Himself who defines the worth and value of women? And, therefore, should not women turn away from the sensuous, degrading definitions of "beauty" that are forced on them by a perverse, shameful culture, and towards God's own definition of "beauty" for women? And thus should not women fear God? And should not those unmarried men who are seeking wives for themselves (that is, who are not called by God to a consecration unto singleness), be seeking only the kind of wives who truly fear the Lord? For, is not *the fear of God* the mark of true, feminine beauty?

> *Charm is deceitful and beauty is passing,*
> *but **a woman who fears the LORD,***
> *she shall be praised.* (Proverbs 31:30)

True womanhood cannot be defined apart from the God of Scripture, the God of Abraham, Isaac, and Jacob. For He alone is the Creator of all, both men and women, and thus we rightly know ourselves only when we repent of our sins (which damage our ability to think clearly and rationally about God and about ourselves), call upon His name for salvation, and thus come to know Him. In the knowledge of God the Father, which comes only through the knowledge of Christ Jesus, His Son, we come to know ourselves. Therefore, women are only able to understand their womanhood by worshipping Christ, through being born again—born of His Holy Spirit. And men are only able to value and love women in their womanhood, chiefly, by directing them into their glorious submission to Christ. Thus men ought to encourage women, with great love and gentleness, to submit themselves to Christ through the knowledge of His holy Word, through fellowship with Him in daily, habitual prayer, and through obedience to His holy commandments, both in total and in their specific applications to women.

It Is a Glory to Her

2

PORNOGRAPHY IS MISOGYNIST

GOD loves women. Therefore, He *hates* pornography. Of course, pornographic images of women would not exist without women volunteering to pose for them (or else being forced to do so, which is a form of the capital crime of rape). Those women who volunteer for this (either for pecuniary interests or for the act of gaining power over men) are, indeed, guilty of great crimes against God. Even if in image only, they are prostituting themselves out to evil men:

> *The daughter of any priest, if she*
> ***profanes herself by playing the harlot***,
> *she profanes her father. She shall be burned with*
> *fire.* (Leviticus 21:9)

Yet men who employ their eyes in the viewing of pornography are guilty of woman-hating crimes.[iii] For, the nature of pornography is a dehumanizing one. It views women as concubines and prostitutes, rather than as God's image bearers, created by God to be protected, treasured, and loved by men with gentle, humble, pure, and sacrificial love.

Pornography mocks the sacredness of the marriage covenant. It defaces the dignity of women. It strips women of their highest honor, which is their holiness before God and their quiet, meek modesty before Him. In the end, therefore, pornography evokes the furious wrath of God, since it treats those who were once precious little girls, wearing toddler shoes and holding toy baby dolls in their arms, *as slaves and temple prostitutes in the worship of the modern goddess Hedonism*.

It is no wonder, then, that God warns men who are patrons of pornography that unless they repent of this sin, and cease from it—by the power of the new birth in the Holy Spirit, through faith in Christ Jesus—they will *not* enter the Kingdom of Heaven:

Do you not know that the unrighteous will not inherit the Kingdom of God? Do not be deceived. **Neither fornicators** *[including users of pornography], nor idolaters,* **nor adulterers** *[also including users of pornography], nor homosexuals, nor sodomites, nor thieves, nor covetous, nor drunkards, nor revilers, nor extortioners* **will inherit the Kingdom of God.**
(1 Corinthians 6:9–10)

Sin is not external only. It is very much internal. The sins of the heart are *vile* in the sight of God. And lust is amongst the worst of them. For, lust is, by nature, both an act of violence against God's commandments concerning the exclusivity of the marriage covenant (since it, by way of internal desire, introduces a foreign "other" into that God-ordained exclusivity) and an act of hatred towards women (since it violently removes the protection of the glory of womanhood that is commanded by Holy Scripture to come through a man's deep, God-fearing earnestness for the *propriety* and *modesty* of all women). It is no wonder, then, that Jesus warns all men vehemently, and in the language of true Hellfire, against the sin of lust:

> *You have heard that it was said to those of old, "You shall not commit adultery." But I say to you that **whoever looks at a woman to lust for her has already committed adultery with her in his heart**. If your right eye causes you to sin, pluck it out and cast it from you; for it is more profitable for you that one of your members perish, **than for your whole body to be cast into Hell**. And if your right hand causes you to sin, cut it off and cast it from you; for it is more profitable for you that one of your members perish, **than for your whole body to be cast into Hell**.* (Matthew 5:27-30)

Moreover, when the Lord Jesus speaks against the sin of pornography, He does so with the burning heat of divine anger and wrath. For, pornography not only builds adultery into the heart of a man, but also brings his *eyes* into *physical* contact with the woman of harlotry. Though it involves a physical image only, yet it is still a physical act. Thus that grave warning of wisdom concerning the deadly dangers of the harlot's house, recounted in the book of Proverbs by a loving father to his youthful son, very much applies to the act of viewing pornography:

*With [the harlot's] enticing speech she caused him to yield, with her flattering lips she seduced him. Immediately he went after her, as an ox goes to the slaughter, or as a fool to the correction of the stocks, till an arrow struck his liver. As a bird hastens to the snare, he did not know it would cost his life. Now therefore, listen to me, my children; pay attention to the words of my mouth. Do not let your heart turn aside to her ways, do not stray into her paths; for she has cast down many wounded, and all who were slain by her were strong men. **Her house is the way to Hell,** descending to the chambers of death.*
(Proverbs 7:21–27)

For married men, this is tantamount to adultery, real adultery. For, the Greek word *porneía*, which describes the kind of *"sexual immorality"* that adulterously shatters a marriage covenant, and thus is divine-legal grounds for divorce, encompasses a host of sexual sins (prostitution, unchastity, fornication, etc.) that certainly include the act of intentionally viewing pornography. (Again, joining oneself to a prostitute [through an illicit conjugation] and intentionally gazing upon the nakedness of a prostitute [through pornography] are the same sin, only committed in different degrees.)[iv] Thus although marital reconciliation through the Gospel is always desirable, whenever possible, nevertheless in certain circumstances, which must be discerned with extreme caution, a woman is no longer spiritually bound to her marriage covenant with a man who has shattered it through his pornographic adulteries. This should cause all married men to tremble, with godly fear:

*And I say to you, whoever divorces his wife, **except for sexual immorality** [Greek: porneía], and marries another, commits adultery; and whoever marries her who is divorced commits adultery.* (Matthew 19:9)

Pornography, then, has the adulterous potential to shatter the marriage covenant of a married man (it does, in fact, *constitute an act of adultery*), and it makes any man—whether married or single—in danger of the unquenchable fires of Hell:

*And if **your eye** causes you to sin, pluck it out. **It is better for you to enter the Kingdom of God with one eye, rather than having two eyes, to be cast into Hell fire**—where: "Their worm does not die and the fire is not quenched."*
(Mark 9:47–48)

O fellow Man (for I speak here in serious man-to-man conversation): do you actually desire the ruin of your own soul, which shall be effected by your eating of the forbidden fruit of pornography? If you are single, are you desirous to be known by God as the perverse patron of such an extreme form of misogyny? If you are married, do you go so far as to desire the harlot of pornography at the expense of the heart of the wife of your youth and the calamitous destruction of your own marriage? If pornography is, as you say it is, an epidemic of sin in society, should you excuse yourself for indulging in it simply because it is an epidemic? If the plague brings death in epidemic proportions, should you seek out the plague for yourself? Are you so captivated by your own lusts that you care not whether your physical flesh will burn with the itchings and pains of everlasting torments in Hell, so long as you can indulge those lustful passions in the wicked, existential moment of the present?

Many, many men in our world are sinfully addicted to pornography at the present time. Yet there is the hope of deliverance through the Gospel of Jesus Christ. Therefore, O fellow Man, if you are one of those who are guilty of walking, willfully (for it was your own will, and thus your own wickedness), into the harlot's house, wherein your mind has been enslaved by her and your soul has been flayed by her, there is an escape door through which you can flee! It is called the Door of Repentance, and on its outside panel are written the words, "Faith in God's Holy Promises."

If you *ask* for the Holy Spirit's power to hate this sin, and to crucify it (unto death, so that it is dead to you) in your life, and *seek* forgiveness of this sin solely upon the merits of Christ's atoning blood and Christ's spotless righteousness alone, and *knock* that this door of escape might be opened for you, and all of this with true grieving and mourning and lamenting before God—tearing your heart, and not merely your garment, in repentance—and with a broken, contrite humility before God, trusting Him, and loving Him truly, then He shall send the power of His grace to bring about your exodus out of this horrific captivity to sin. In turn, having been set free from slavery to sin, you shall rejoice to become a slave to righteousness—a happy slave to righteousness!—being transformed by the renewing of your mind, and finding verses of Scripture such as 1 Timothy 5:2, *"[Treat] older women as mothers, [and] younger women as sisters, with all purity,"* to be so full of the sweetness and goodness of God's life-giving holiness in you that you no longer have any perverse craving for the filthy sins of your former way of life.

Men instituted the wickedness of pornography, and, therefore, *men* must lead the way towards its abolition from all human society. Thus once pornography is exposed for the misogyny that it is, we ought to see men taking up spiritual arms against it. There ought to be Christ-honoring men boycotting sports stadiums on account of the way in which the sports team owners pay cheerleaders to dress like prostitutes, thus tempting young men and dehumanizing young women.[v] There also ought to be men who fear God to such an extent that they will *not* expose their eyes *even to a single* movie, television show, or internet video that contains any measure of blatant immodesty, since to do so would be to join their eyes with the harlotry of today's video culture of image-driven prostitution.

Those men who are yoked to Christ, since they

are under the fear of Christ and His warnings about the adultery of the heart, should not direct their eyes in public, even with a glance, towards immodestly dressed women, anywhere, at any time. Certainly, Christian men in society should work tirelessly for the legal abolition of pornography, since to abolish pornography via the law of the land, and to ensure the just enforcement of the law, would be to effect one of the greatest moral-political reformations of the contemporary age.[vi]

Likewise, O valuable Woman, created in God's image (for I speak here to those women who consciences testify to them that they are, indeed, created in God's image *as distinctly feminine*), do not allow men treat you like a prostitute (coaxing you into acts of immodesty outside of the covenant of marriage). Also, do not let "fashion" tell you that you have to dress like one. (For, modern fashion is so immodest that it does, indeed, demand that women dress like harlots.) Do not do it! For, if you do allow the misogyny of the pornographic spirit of the age to drag you into the female sins of immodesty, seduction, and the usurpation of ruling authority (a ruling authority which properly belongs to men), you only will find that the "Sexual Revolution" was a revolt unto sexual bondage (and oppression and abuse), not freedom, and that the Feminist lifestyle of "Women's Liberation" results not in true liberation, but in slavery to career, pride, deception, and all of the mangling distortions of heart and identity that come about when masculinity is pressed and stamped, industrial style, upon the minds and bodies of women.

O dignified Woman, created by God for the glory of purity! Do you want to be treated like a prostitute by the man whom you shall marry? Do you not, rather, want to be treated as a daughter of the Lord God, and thus as a princess in the Kingdom of Christ Jesus? If so, settle for nothing less than a truly God-fearing man. Find the man who will save the first kiss for your wedding day, and who will be zealous for your holiness—guarding it vigilantly with the Word of God. Yet make sure, also, that he is very meek and gentle. For, he must treat you with love and gentleness, sacrificing himself for you just as Christ loved the Church and sacrificed Himself for the Church, and he must love children—much like a shepherd who loves to hold the nursing lambs in his arms.

IT IS A GLORY TO HER

3

PURITY IS PRECIOUS

GOD loves women. Therefore, *purity* is precious, for by purity men protect and value women, and by purity women complement and honor men. Yet *all* are sinners, since *all* humans (except Christ Jesus) sin, and thus the preciousness of purity in the lives of all people cannot be obtained apart from the forgiveness of sins. That is, no matter how "righteous" a man might seem in his own eyes, his sins against God have made his soul stained by sinful filth, the wicked deeds of a child of wrath, and thus worthy of everlasting condemnation in the torments of Hell:

> *But we are all like an unclean thing, and **all our righteousnesses are like filthy rags**; we all fade as a leaf, and our iniquities, like the wind, have taken us away.* (Isaiah 64:6)

Yet praise be to God, through Christ Jesus our Lord, that there is a way to be made pure! If you will but repent, and turn away from your former allegiances to Satan and to sin, and believe in the name of the Son of God, you shall be saved from your sinful filthiness. For it is with the heart that you *believe in Him*, and thus obtain righteousness *by faith in Him*, and it is with the mouth that you confess, *"Jesus is Lord"* [Jesus is the Lord GOD, the Creator of all things, the Lord of Heaven and earth, who alone has the divine right to rule and reign over your own heart] unto salvation.

Then—grace upon grace!—Christ Jesus takes you, the former spiritual adulterer or adulteress (and all people are guilty of committing spiritual adultery against God through their worship of idols), and clothes you in pristine garments of righteousness:

> *Then one of the elders answered, saying to me, "Who are these arrayed in **white robes**, and where did they come from?" And I said to him, "Sir, you know." So he said to me, "These are the ones who come out of the great tribulation, and washed their robes and **made them white in the blood of the Lamb**."* (Revelation 7:13–14)

What, then, are we saved from sin so that we can continue reveling in sin, without future punishment? By no means! Instead, when we are saved, we die to sin with Christ's death on the cross, and we rise, born of His Holy Spirit, unto newness of life. Thus we are born anew, empowered by the Spirit of Christ to die to sin and live for righteousness, since by His wounds we have been healed. We are, then, saved unto a life of *purity* and *holiness*:

Therefore, having these promises, beloved, let us
cleanse ourselves from all filthiness
of the flesh and spirit, **perfecting holiness**
in the fear of God. (2 Corinthians 7:1)

In fact, growth in holiness, as evidenced by the fruits of the Holy Spirit, an ever-increasing hatred of sin, and an ever-increasing love of righteousness, is the mark of true salvation (as opposed to a false claim of having been born of Christ):

Pursue peace with all people, **and holiness, without**
which no one will see the Lord.
(Hebrews 12:14)

Therefore, it is only through the Gospel of Jesus Christ, the Son of God, that women can labor to regain the glory of their own womanhood, and that men can toil to restore the glory of womanhood to women (which, being negligent in their leadership and ravenous in their lusts, ungodly men have stripped from women). And what is that glory? Is it not God-fearing modesty, marked by God-fearing submission?[vii]

I desire therefore that…the women adorn themselves
in **modest apparel***, with propriety and moderation.*
(1 Timothy 2:8-9)

*Do not let your adornment be merely outward— arranging the hair, wearing gold, or putting on fine apparel—rather let it be the hidden person of the heart, with **the incorruptible beauty of a gentle and quiet spirit**, which is very **precious** in the sight of God.* (1 Peter 3:3–4)

*...to be **discreet, chaste, homemakers, good, obedient to their own husbands**, that the Word of God may not be blasphemed.* (Titus 2:5)

A woman's covering of submission is her crown, her glory. As she submits herself, like Mary, meekly unto God, she finds herself covered with the strong, divine protection and brilliant, Heavenly light of the love of Christ Jesus for her. Walking in the way of the women who feared the Lord throughout the history of the Church,[viii] she covers her head in public, for that sign of submission on her is for her glory, under God's love:

***Let her be covered*.*…It is *a glory* to her.** (1 Corinthians 11:6, 15)

In the same manner, the glory of manhood, man's headship, which, as ordained by God, commands respect and honor, comes only through his sacrificial protection of, sacrificial provision for, and sacrificial love rendered unto women, all for the glory of God. In other words, if a man wisely and rightly flees today's rampant homosexualization of manhood, knowing it to be one of the worst of all abominations in the sight of God (for homosexuality is one of the greatest wickednesses in the history of human rebellion against God),[ix] he nevertheless does not attain to true manhood unless he submits himself to the fear of God, and in that holy fear learns to fight for the glory of womanhood by doing everything in his strength (and yet it is Christ's strength at work through him) to promote the purity of his Christian sisters before God:

*Husbands, **love your** wives, just as Christ also loved the Church and gave Himself for her, that He might sanctify and cleanse her with the washing of water by the Word, that He might present her to Himself a glorious Church, **not having spot or wrinkle or any such thing, but that she should be holy and without blemish**.* (Ephesians 5:25–27)

A word, then, specifically to Christian men: beloved Christian Brother, are you protecting the purity of women in society and in the Church, even by calling them to shun the ravenous idols of Feminism that are seeking to devour them? Are you calling your fellow men to repent of their misogynist lusts, lewd speech, and life-damaging immoralities perpetrated against women? Are you upholding the utmost holiness, propriety, and gentleness in all of your treatment of women? Also, are you waging spiritual warfare against the sin of birth control, and all of the monstrous evils that it has perpetrated against women, both unmarried and married alike?

Moreover, O God-fearing man, are you providing constant encouragements for the Christian women in your home, saturated with Scripture, concerning the value and beauty of a God-fearing, God-centered life? Are you cheering for them as they run with perseverance the race of pious, feminine purity? If so, valiant Brother, your meek, foot-washing example, executed with Gospel tears over the sexual abuse of women in the Church and in society, is a labor of love that is not in done in vain. It shall have its great reward in the Kingdom of Heaven.

And a final word to the women of the Church: O precious Sister! This is what is truly precious: to be covered with modesty, and clothed with godliness. It is precious to treasure God's Word in your heart, to meditate upon it day and night, to adorn yourself with good works for the afflicted and the needy (and thus to be a public voice of intercession for the little ones of the Abortion Holocaust), and to walk worthy of the Lord, fully pleasing Him, being fruitful in every good work, and increasing in the knowledge of God. In this manner, precious Sister, you will be a radiant and lovely daughter of the Lord, much like a beautiful pillar in God's Temple, *"sculptured in palace style"* (Psalm 144:12).

Purity is precious! In Heaven, it shall be a mark of everlasting glory upon the Church. For whom did Christ die? He died for His Bride, the Church. For whom shall Christ return? He shall return for His Bride, the Church, since He is jealous for her.

He desires her purity; He has given His own

blood for her, in order to wash her and sanctify her in His blood. He has betrothed her to Himself as a chaste virgin. Christ Jesus has purposed to be her Lord, that she would worship Him, and that in worshipping Him she would be made radiant, wearing a wedding gown woven with gold and being adorned in garments of many colors, so that He Himself might greatly desire her beauty.

Even at present, she is beautified by the Holy Spirit, like a lily among thorns. Yet in Heaven, she shall be to Him as a lily ever blooming, and everlastingly fragrant, without any thorns surrounding her at all. When He comes, He shall bring her to His great feast, the marriage supper of the Lamb, and there she shall be clothed in fine linen, clean and bright, full of righteousness, precious in purity. And thus the Lamb shall have His Bride, in purity, and all the saints shall see His glory, for the tabernacle of God shall be with them, and He will dwell with them, and they shall be His people, and God Himself will be with them and be their God. Amen.

IT IS A GLORY TO HER

NOTES

[i] Frank L. Houghton, *Amy Carmichael of Dohnavur* (The Dohnavur Fellowship, 1954; repr., Fort Washington, PA: Christian Literature Crusade, 2004), 138.

[ii] Qtd. in Ibid., 142.

[iii] In this regard, note 1 Peter 4:3-4: *"For **we have spent enough of our past lifetime** in doing the will of the Gentiles—when **we walked in lewdness, lusts, drunkenness, revelries, drinking parties, and abominable idolatries**. In regard to these, they think it strange that you do not run with them in the same flood of dissipation, speaking evil of you."*

[iv] No doubt, joining oneself to a prostitute constitutes a sin of higher degree than intentionally viewing pornography, and thus a greater adultery, but nevertheless, for a married man, the two sins are both very much "adulterous."

[v] Christ-honoring men should boycott the collegiate and professional sports stadiums not only on account of their prostitute-attired cheerleaders, but also on account of the *idolatry of sports* that takes place within them. Also, regarding other known places of public immodesty, at which women are encouraged to dress in public with a "norm" of gross immodesty (for example, at most American beach fronts on warm, sunny days), Christ-honoring men should purposefully avoid such places, so long as the "norm" of public immodesty persists at them.

[vi] Here, instead of following the faulty argument of the extreme Dispensationalists, who say that we "should not try to legislate morality," and that only the preaching of the Gospel, for salvation, will do, we agree with William Wilberforce that *"from law* arises security" in a nation, and that God desires such (moral) security, through the knowledge of His holy commandments, in all nations (William Wilberforce, *A Letter on the Abolition of the Slave Trade: Addressed to the Freeholders and other Inhabitants of Yorkshire* [London: Luke Hansard & Sons, 1807], 73). Then, this biblical law, once translated into political law through the Gospel, becomes *a means by which the Gospel is proclaimed* (e.g. the call for the abolition of pornography in society is simultaneously a call to repent from all of the sins of the heart associated with pornography, and thus to believe the Gospel and be saved from the wrath to come).

[vii] The specifics of practical submission in the life of a godly woman must be worked out through a true interpretation of, and a humble

obedience to such passages as: Proverbs 31:10-31; Luke 1:38; Acts 9:36; 1 Corinthians 11:1-16; Ephesians 5:22-24; Colossians 3:18; 1 Timothy 2:9-15; Titus 2:3-5; etc.

viii Regarding the command for all Christian women, in all cultures, to wear a head covering in public, note that Paul writes, with authority, *"But if anyone seems to be contentious, we have no such custom, nor do the churches of God"* (1 Corinthians 11:16). Also, note that the ancient Church Fathers consistently and unanimously affirmed the commandment as a timeless one, not at all bound by culture or place. Lastly, consider carefully the clairvoyance built into the following words of John Calvin, "*...when it [becomes] permissible for the women to uncover their heads, one will say, 'Well, what harm in uncovering the stomach also?' And then after that one will plead [for] something else: 'Now if the women go bareheaded, why not also [bare] this and [bare] that?' Then the men, for their part, will break loose too. ....So if women are thus permitted to have their heads uncovered and to show their hair, they will eventually be allowed to expose their entire breasts, and they will come to make their exhibitions as if it were a tavern show. ....In short, there will be no decency left, unless people contain themselves and respect what is proper and fitting, so as not to go headlong overboard*" (Calvin, Sermon on 1 Corinthians 11:2-3 in *Men, Women and Order in the Church*, trans Seth Skolnitsky, Presbyterian Heritage Publications, pp. 12-13).

ix Jude, the brother of Jesus, calls God's act of sending fire from Heaven upon Sodom and Gomorrah, on account of their *"sexual immorality"* and the *"strange flesh"* of their homosexuality, a mere, smaller *"example"* of the greater, future judgment of those who persist, without true repentance, in their homosexuality—a future, final state of judgment which will be filled with *"the vengeance of eternal fire"* (Jude 7).

www.ingramcontent.com/pod-product-compliance
Lightning Source LLC
Chambersburg PA
CBHW060546030426
42337CB00021B/4459